Jt Lewis and Clark

by Lisa Moore
illustrated by Tom McNeely

Harcourt
SCHOOL PUBLISHERS

Requests for permission to make copies of any part of the work should be addressed to School Permissions and Copyrights, Harcourt, Inc., 6277 Sea Harbor Drive, Orlando, Florida 32887–6777. Fax: 407-345-2418.

HARCOURT and the Harcourt Logo are trademarks of Harcourt, Inc., registered in the United States of America and/or other jurisdictions.

Printed in Mexico

ISBN 10: 0-15-350296-7
ISBN 13: 978-0-15-350296-5

Ordering Options
ISBN 10: 0-15-349940-0 (Grade 5 ELL Collection)
ISBN 13: 978-0-15-349940-1 (Grade 5 ELL Collection)
ISBN 10: 0-15-357335-X (package of 5)
ISBN 13: 978-0-15-357335-4 (package of 5)

2 3 4 5 6 7 8 9 10   126   12 11 10 09 08 07

The Miller family is going camping. The two children, Sierra and Jasper, have never been camping before. They are going with their parents to a place called Cape Disappointment State Park.

Sierra and Jasper's father loves to read about Lewis and Clark. They were two explorers who hiked hundreds of miles from St. Louis, Missouri, to the West Coast in 1805. Cape Disappointment is the place where Lewis and Clark reached the Pacific Ocean. The park is in what is now the state of Washington. Papa has been talking about this camping trip for months.

Sierra and Jasper go over the checklist. They bring sleeping bags, lanterns, a tent, and other supplies. Sierra is excited. Jasper yawns. He thinks camping is a waste of time.

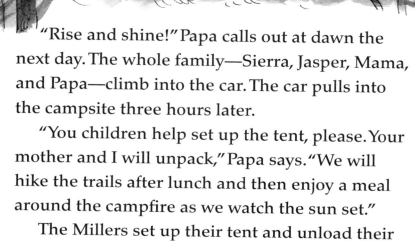

"Rise and shine!" Papa calls out at dawn the next day. The whole family—Sierra, Jasper, Mama, and Papa—climb into the car. The car pulls into the campsite three hours later.

"You children help set up the tent, please. Your mother and I will unpack," Papa says. "We will hike the trails after lunch and then enjoy a meal around the campfire as we watch the sun set."

The Millers set up their tent and unload their car. Then they sit at the picnic table and eat peanut butter sandwiches and apples. The family members fill their water bottles, strap on their backpacks, and set out for the trails.

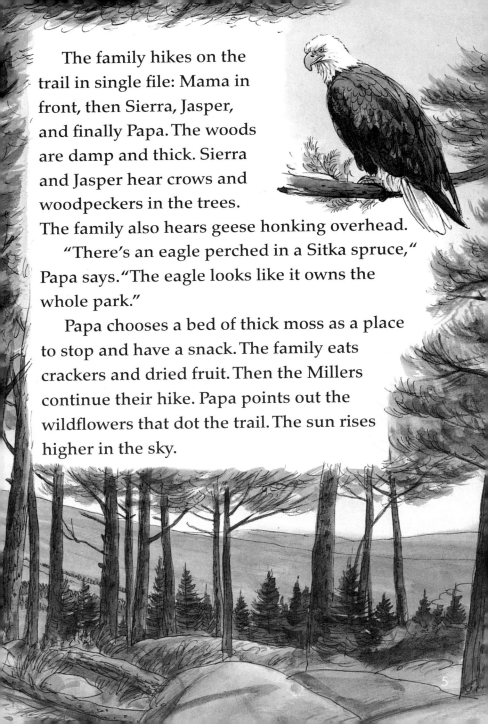

The family hikes on the trail in single file: Mama in front, then Sierra, Jasper, and finally Papa. The woods are damp and thick. Sierra and Jasper hear crows and woodpeckers in the trees. The family also hears geese honking overhead.

"There's an eagle perched in a Sitka spruce," Papa says. "The eagle looks like it owns the whole park."

Papa chooses a bed of thick moss as a place to stop and have a snack. The family eats crackers and dried fruit. Then the Millers continue their hike. Papa points out the wildflowers that dot the trail. The sun rises higher in the sky.

Soon the Millers see the Pacific coast before them. The view is amazing. Waves splash against the rocks. Seagulls squawk and circle. Then the family returns to the campsite. Mama builds a campfire. Sierra and her brother collect wood.

"What do you think of camping?" Mama asks her children.

"It's good," Jasper and Sierra answer.

The sun sets. The Millers eat fish, roasted vegetables, and baked potatoes that were cooked in the fire. The food tastes great. The family roasts marshmallows over the open campfire for dessert. Papa talks about Lewis and Clark.

"Lewis and Clark and their group traveled a long way, over mountains and across rivers. These people must have been so happy when they arrived at this place," Papa says. His eyes sparkle in the glow of the campfire. "These people hiked for years and faced so much danger. The trip was long and difficult. Finally, Lewis and Clark found what they had been looking for— the Pacific Ocean."

Soon it's time for the Millers to say good night. They put out the campfire with water. They brush their teeth. "Put all the food in the car," Papa warns. "There may be raccoons out here."

Sierra stares at her brother in fear. He laughs and crawls into the tent. Mama turns off the lantern. Everyone snuggles into a sleeping bag. Sierra can't see her hand when she holds it in front of her face because of the darkness. Soon she falls asleep.

Sierra wakes during the night when she hears a sound outside. She hits the button on her watch that lights up the dial. It's almost four o'clock in the morning. "Jasper!" she whispers. "Jasper, did you hear that?"

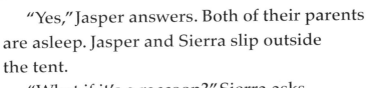

"Yes," Jasper answers. Both of their parents are asleep. Jasper and Sierra slip outside the tent.

"What if it's a raccoon?" Sierra asks.

Outside, there is moonlight. Millions of stars fill the night sky. Jasper stares at the sky. He can't believe there are so many stars. The sky is better than television. It's better than the Internet. It's bigger and better than anything Jasper has ever seen before.

"Let's sleep right outside the tent," Sierra says.

"What about that noise?" Jasper asks.

"It's nothing," Sierra says. "If it was a raccoon it's gone now."

Sierra reaches in the tent for their sleeping bags. She throws Jasper's pillow at him. He catches it, smiling. Sierra and Jasper sleep under millions of stars. They dream about Lewis and Clark's adventures.

At dawn, Sierra awakens and sees something out of the corner of her eye. A fawn is looking at her from across the way. Sierra stares at the young deer's soft brown eyes until the fawn runs into the woods. Sierra turns to Jasper who is awake and looks very surprised.

Soon their parents climb out of the tent. "Wow, what a morning!" Papa exclaims. "Just like—"

"We know. We know," Mama says. "Just like Lewis and Clark must have seen." Papa smiles.

Sierra helps her parents build a new campfire and make breakfast. Jasper sits on a nearby rock. He writes in his journal.

"Do you still think camping is a waste of time?" Sierra asks Jasper at breakfast. The Millers are eating oatmeal and drinking hot tea. Jasper's hair is messy. He sits with his sleeping bag around his shoulders.

"No," is all he says.

"What did you write this morning?" Sierra asks. "I saw you with your journal."

Jasper frowns. He doesn't usually share his writing. However, today he grabs his journal from the picnic table. He begins to read.

A New Hobby

I didn't want to go camping.
I didn't want to sleep in a tent.
I didn't want a campfire
with its ash and smoky scent.

Then I saw a million stars
shining in a coal black sky.
I was very happy that
I'd given camping a try.

I heard the Pacific Ocean
the way Lewis and Clark once did.
I hid in the trees to see an eagle
the way Lewis and Clark once hid.

When I saw a fawn,
sniffing the morning mist,
I knew that I'd add camping
to my favorite hobbies list!

Everyone is smiling when Jasper finishes reading his poem. The ocean roars in the distance. A woodpecker *tap, tap, taps* in the trees above.

The Millers break down their campsite. They pack up their tent. They load their car. Each of them thinks about Lewis and Clark, about Jasper's poem, and about the long drive home.

"Next time, let's camp out for two or three nights," Jasper says. "One night is not enough." The rest of the family agrees.

Scaffolded Language Development

USING CAPITAL LETTERS Point out the words *Miller, Lewis, Clark,* and *Cape Disappointment State Park* on page 3. Ask students what they all have in common. If necessary, tell students they all start with capital letters and are proper nouns. A proper noun names a specific person, a place, or a thing.

Ask students to capitalize the proper nouns in the following sentences:

1. Last year my family went to new york city.
2. We saw the statue of liberty.
3. A man named frederic bartholdi created the statue.
4. He was a sculptor from france.
5. He gave the statue as a gift to the united states of america.

Social Studies

Sacagawea Tell students that Lewis and Clark were greatly helped by a Native American woman named Sacagawea. Have them research more background information on Sacagawea and how she helped the explorers. Ask students to write a short report summarizing their findings.

School-Home Connection

Explorers Have students share with family members what they have learned about Sacagawea. Suggest that they talk about women today who have traits in common with Sacagawea.

Word Count: 1,124